Rookie
Read-About® Geography

Map Scales

WITHDRAWN

By Mary Dodson Wade

Consultant
Jeanne Clidas, Ph.D.
National Reading Consultant
and
Professor of Reading, SUNY Brockport

Children's Press®
A Division of Scholastic Inc.
New York   Toronto   London   Auckland   Sydney
Mexico City   New Delhi   Hong Kong
Danbury, Connecticut

Designer: Herman Adler Design
Photo Researcher: Caroline Anderson
The artwork on the cover shows a simple map and corresponding scale.

Library of Congress Cataloging-in-Publication Data

Wade, Mary Dodson.
  Map scales / by Mary Dodson Wade.
    p. cm. — (Rookie read-about geography)
Includes index.
  ISBN 0-516-22720-3 (lib. bdg.)   0-516-27767-7 (pbk.)
  1. Map scales—Juvenile literature. [1. Introduces how to determine
approximately how far apart places are by using the scale on a map.
2. Map reading. 3. Maps.] I. Title. II. Series.
  GA118 .W34 2003
  912'.01'48—dc21
                                        2002011536

CHILDREN'S PRESS, AND ROOKIE READ-ABOUT®,
and associated logos are trademarks and or registered trademarks
of Grolier Publishing Co., Inc. SCHOLASTIC and associated logos
are trademarks and or registered trademarks of Scholastic Inc.

1 2 3 4 5 6 7 8 9 10 R 12 11 10 09 08 07 06 05 04 03

There are scales on fish
and scales for weighing
(WAY-ing) fruit. What kind
of scales do maps have?

3

Maps have scales that help you read the map.

The map scale helps you measure (MEZH-ur) how far away something is.

The scale is a line that stands for a certain distance (DISS-tuhnss).

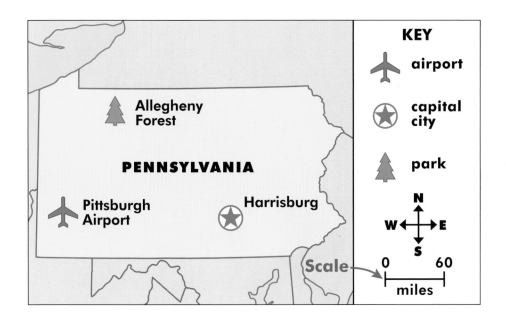

KEY

✈ airport

⊛ capital city

🌲 park

N
W — E
S

Scale

0   60

miles

5

MAP KEY

 airport

 capital city

 park

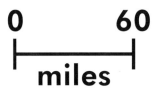

0   60

miles

Every map has a map scale line. The line is located inside a box called a map key or legend (LEG-uhnd). The legend can be found on the side, top, or bottom of the map.

Also inside the map key box are symbols (SIM-buhlz). These symbols stand for places on the map.

Where is the airport on this map?

Trees show where a park can be found.

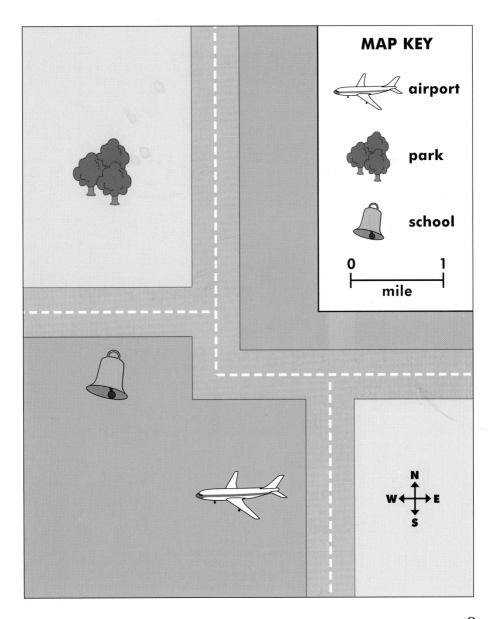

MAP KEY

✈ airport

🌳 park

🔔 school

0 — 1
mile

N
W ← → E
S

9

MAP KEY

airport

park

school

0   1
|——————————————|
mile

The distance covered by the map scale line changes with each map. This scale line stands for one mile.

On a map of a country, the line might stand for 200 miles.

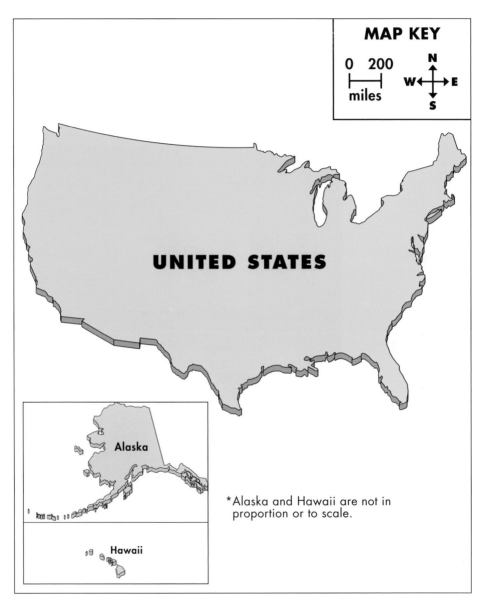

MAP KEY

0   200
miles

N
W — E
S

UNITED STATES

Alaska

Hawaii

*Alaska and Hawaii are not in proportion or to scale.

13

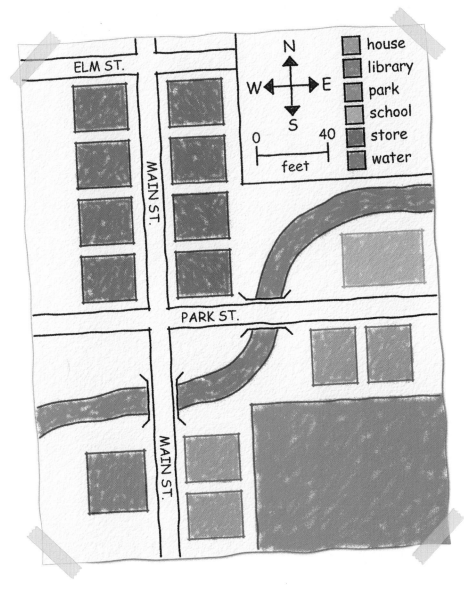

ELM ST.

MAIN ST.

PARK ST.

MAIN ST.

N
W E
S

0   40
feet

house
library
park
school
store
water

14

On a map of the block
where you live, the line
might stand for 40 feet.

When you read a map, look at the map scale line. Do you see the number at the end of the line? It shows how many feet or miles the line stands for.

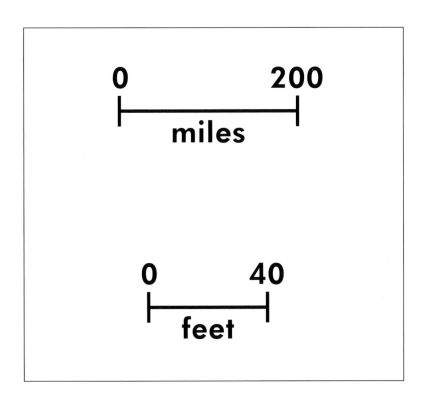

0   200

miles

0   40

feet

0   **200**

miles

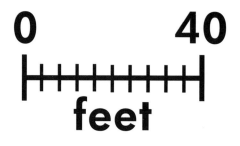

0   **40**

feet

Little marks divide up the line. These marks show shorter distances.

Here is a map of a zoo.
Find the giraffe's house
and the polar bear's
swimming pool.

Use your ruler to measure
the map scale line. It is
one inch long.

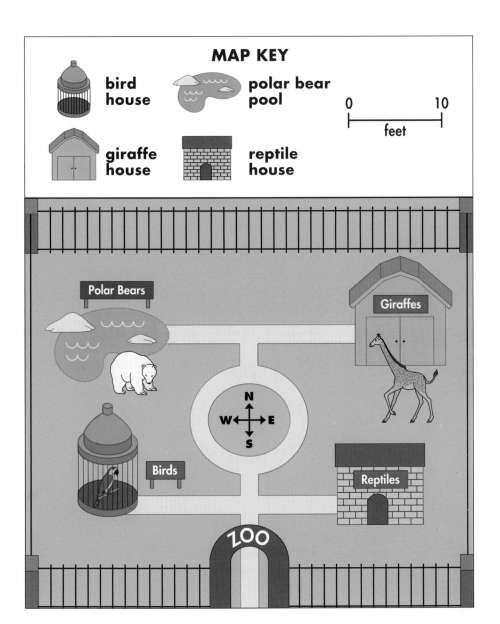

21

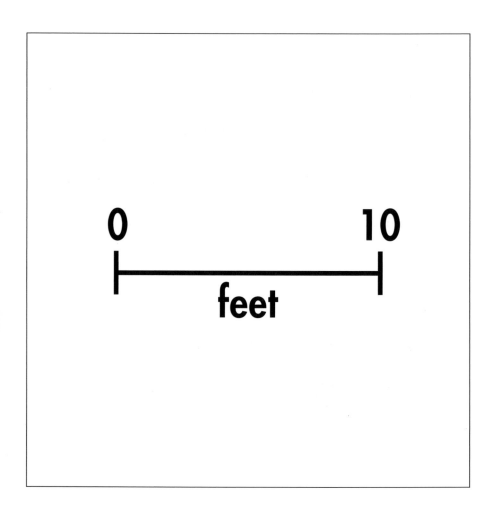

0   10

feet

22

Now look at the number at the end of the map scale line. It shows you that one inch stands for 10 feet.

How far is the giraffe's house from the polar bear's pool?

Use your ruler to measure the distance. Did you measure two inches?

The giraffe's house and the polar bear's pool are two inches apart on the map.

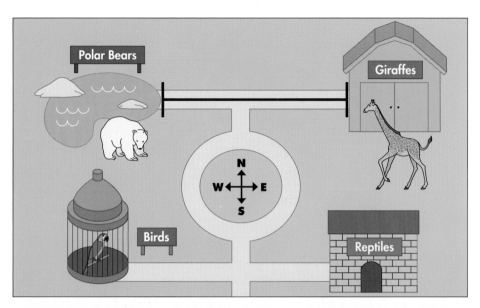

25

How far apart are they at the zoo?

Add 10 feet plus 10 feet and you will know the distance between the giraffe's house and the polar bear's pool.

Answer: 20 feet

A map scale helps you figure out the distance between places on a map.

How can this help you?

Words You Know

giraffe

MAP KEY

airport

park

school

0   1
mile

map key

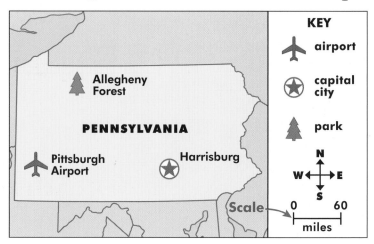

map

30

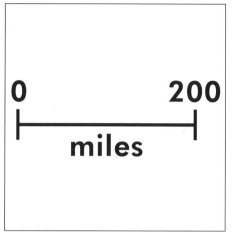

map scale line

polar bear

ruler

park

school

symbols

31

Index

About the Author

Mary Dodson Wade spent 25 years as an elementary school teacher, but she has been writing even longer than that, starting with poems as a child. She has had more than 20 books published. Mary and her husband live in Houston, Texas, and love to travel.

Photo Credits